KUMARA-SAMBHAVA

OF

-KALIDASA

AF512813

CANTO III

Edited with introduction and English translation

C.R. DEVADHAR

MOTILAL BANARSIDASS
PUBLISHERS PRIVATE LIMITED •
DELHI

First Edition: Delhi, 1985
Reprint: Delhi, 1989, 2000

© MOTILAL BANARSIDASS PUBLISHERS PVT. LTD.
All Rights Reserved

Also available at:

MOTILAL BANARSIDASS

41 U.A. Bungalow Road, Jawahar Nagar, Delhi 110 007 8
Mahalaxmi Chamber, Warden Road, Mumbai 400 026
120 Royapettah High Road, Mylapore, Chennai 600 004
236, 9th Main III Block, Jayanagar, Bangalore 560 011
Sanas Plaza, 1302 Baji Rao Road, Pune 411 002
8 Camac Street, Calcutta 700 017
Ashok Rajpath, Patna 800 004
Chowk, Varanasi 221 001

Printed in India
BY JAINENDRA PRAKASH JAIN AT SHRI JAINENDRA PRESS,
A-45 NARAINA INDUSTRIAL AREA, PHASE I, NEW DELHI 110 028
AND PUBLISHED BY NARENDRA PRAKASH JAIN FOR
MOTILAL BANARSIDASS PUBLISHERS PRIVATE LIMITED,
BUNGALOW ROAD, DELHI 110 007

INTRODUCTION

The Kumārasambhava of Kālidāsa is a tour-de-force of literary effort of a very high order, and is in fact the oriflamme of Indian poetic genius. It is a gem among Kālidāsa's poetic works. It sings of divine love and of the strife between Tāraka's demon hosts and godly hosts led by Kumāra, in which ultimately Asura Tāraka is worsted. It is based on a legend of the Śivapurāṇa.

Canto—III :—

The thousand eyes of Indra fell upon Kāma, who stood before him with folded hands, and said, 'What do you seek to accomplish in the world ?" Indra replied, 'The gods desire a commander-in-chief to be born out of the seed of Bhava, for victory. I have heard from heavenly nymph that the daughter of the mountain, at the behest of her father, is waiting upon Lord Śiva, who is practising penance upon the upper reaches of the mountain. Try that the self-restrained daughter of Himādri is liked by him. Kāma, accompanied by Rati, went to Śiva's Āśrama. He was also accompanied by his friend Spring, who appeared in the forest. Then approached Pārvatī, accompanied by her friends in the forest, and offered to Śiva a rosary of lotus-seeds. He was about to accept it when the god of love placed a shaft powerful upon his bow. Then Śaṁkara curbed the agitation of his senses with strong will, and looking for its cause, directed his gaze to the ends of the quarters and saw Kāma; Then all at once, a flame of fire shot from his third eye, and consumed Kāma to ashes. Pārvatī felt that her heart's desire was of no availand she was led homewards by Himādri.

तृतीयः सर्गः

तस्मिन्मघोनस्त्रिदशान्विहाय सहस्रमक्ष्णां युगपत्पपात ।
प्रयोजनापेक्षितया प्रभूणां प्रायश्चलं गौरवमाश्रितेषु ॥१॥

The thousand eyes of Indra fell upon Kāma simultaneously; generally, the regard, the masters feel for their servants, is unsteady depending as it does, on their desire to gain their purpose. (1).

स वासवेनासनसन्निकृष्टमितो निषीदेति विसृष्टभूमिः ।
भर्तुः प्रसादं प्रतिनन्द्य मूर्ध्ना वक्तुं मिथः प्राक्रमतैवमेनम् ॥२॥

He was asked by Indra to take his seat near his throne, which Indra pointed out to him; and greeting the favour of his master, (Kāma) proceeded to talk mutually in secret. (2).

आज्ञापय ज्ञातविशेष पुंसां लोकेषु यत्ते करणीयमस्ति ।
अनुग्रहं संस्मरणप्रवृत्तमिच्छामि संवर्द्धितमाज्ञया ते ॥३॥

"Command me, O thou ! that knowest the special merit of men, what thou seekest in the world to accomplish. The favour thou hast shown me by remembering me I desire it to be augmented. (3).

केनाऽभ्यसूया पदकाङ्क्षिणा ते नितान्तदीर्घैर्जनिता तपोभिः ।
यावद्भवत्याहितसायकस्य मत्कामुकस्याऽस्य निदेशवर्ती ॥४॥

Who has inflamed thy wrath by seeking to attain thy position by performing protracted penances ? For he will be soon the target of my bow upon which an arrow is placed. (4).

असंमतः कस्तव मुक्तिमार्गं पुनर्भवक्लेशभयात्प्रपन्नः ।
बद्धश्चिरं तिष्ठतु सुन्दरीणामारेचितभ्रूचतुरैः कटाक्षैः ॥५॥

Whom dost thou abhor ? Who, fearing the agony of rebirth, has taken to the path of salvation ? Let him stand transfixed by the glances of beautiful women, accompanied by the dance of the eye-brow. (5).

अध्यापितस्योशनसापि नीतिं प्रयुक्तरागप्रणिधिर्द्विषस्ते ।
कस्यार्थधर्मौ वद पीडयामि सिन्धोस्तटावोघ इव प्रवृद्धः ॥६॥

Although taught statecraft by Śukra himself, whose worldly goods (Artha) and Dharma shall I block by sending as my emissary, desire for worldly pleasures, as erodes river's bank, its overflooded currents. (6).

कामेकपत्नीव्रतदुःखशीलां लोलं मनश्चारुतया प्रविष्टाम् ।
नितम्बिनीमिच्छसि मुक्तलज्जां कण्ठे स्वयंग्राहनिषक्तबाहुम् ॥७॥

What chaste wife, who suffers pain on account of keeping her vow, who has entered thy fickle heart on account of her beauty, dost thou desire to clasp thy neck in her arms shamelessly, of her own accord? (7).

कयासि कामिन् ! सुरतापराधात्पादानतः कोपनयाऽवधूतः ।
तस्याः करिष्यामि दृढानुतापं प्रवालशय्याशरणं शरीरम् ॥८॥

O thou, love-lorn, by what lady, hast thou been spurned, on account of your faithlessness in love, when fallen prostrate before her, whom I should cause to betake herself to a bed of tender leaves, being full of deep remorse? (8).

प्रसीद विश्राम्यतु वीर ! वज्रं शरैर्मदीयैः कतमः सुरारिः ।
बिभेतु मोघीकृतबाहुवीर्यः स्त्रीभ्योऽपि कोपस्फुरिताधराभ्यः ॥९॥

Be pleased, O hero; let thy thunderbolt rest; what of the enemy of the gods shall I make by my arrow fear women, whose brows are wrinkled in anger, the power of their arms being frustrated? (9).

तव प्रसादात्कुसुमायुधोऽपि सहायमेकं मधुमेव लब्ध्वा ।
कुर्यां हरस्यापि पिनाकपाणेर्धैर्यच्युतिं के मम धन्विनोऽन्ये ॥१०॥

Through thy favour, I even the flower-armed Kāma, with Spring as my only ally, shall make even Pinākin (Śiva) lose courage; other bowmen are nothing before me." (10).

अथोरुदेशादवतार्य पादमाक्रान्तिसम्भावितपादपीठम् ।
सङ्कल्पितार्थे विवृतात्मशक्तिमाखण्डलः काममिदं बभाषे ॥११॥

Then Indra, lowering his foot from a wide region, honoured the foot-stool by planting his foot on it and spoke to Kāma, who had revealed his power in the accomplishment of the desired object, thus :—(11).

सर्वं सखे ! त्वय्युपपन्नमेतदुभे ममाऽस्त्रे कुलिशं भवांश्च ।
वज्रं तपोवीर्यमहत्सु कुण्ठं त्वं सर्वतोगामि च साधकं च ॥१२॥

"Friend, all this is possible for thee; both you and my thunderbolt are my missiles; my thunderbolt is powerless against those who are rich in penance, but thou art ubiquitous and accomplisheth the end. (12).

अवैमि ते सारमतः खलु त्वां कार्ये गुरुण्यात्मसमं नियोक्ष्ये ।
व्यादिश्यते भूधरतामवेक्ष्य कृष्णेन देहोद्वहनाय शेषः ॥१३॥

I know thy strength, and so I appoint thee, my equal, to accomplish a weighty task; Kṛṣṇa, seeing his power to hold the earth makes use of Śeṣa to hold his body. (13).

आशंसता बाणगतिं वृषाङ्के कार्यं त्वया नः प्रतिपन्नकल्पम् ।
निबोध यज्ञांशभुजामिदानीमुच्चैर्द्विषामीप्सितमेतदेव ॥१४॥

Saying that you will direct your arrow's flight towards Śiva, you have almost accomplished our task; know that the gods who have powerful enemies desire nothing else (14).

अमी हि वीर्यप्रभवं भवस्य जयाय सेनान्यमुशन्ति देवाः ।
स च त्वदेकेषुनिपातसाध्यो ब्रह्माङ्गभूर्ब्रह्मणि योजितात्मा ॥१५॥

These gods desire a commander sprung from Hara's seed; he who has concentrated his mind on Brahma, by duly reciting mantra is to be subdued by the fall of only one arrow of yours. (15).

तस्मै हिमाद्रेः प्रयतां तनूजां यतात्मने रोचयितुं यतस्व ।
योषित्सु तद्वीर्यनिषेकभूमिः सैव क्षमेत्यात्मभुवोपदिष्टम् ॥१६॥

Try to induce him whose mind is self-controlled, to be predisposed towards Himādri's self-controlled daughter; for she alone, among women, is capable of bearing his seed; so Brahmā has told. (16).

गुरोर्नियोगाच्च नगेन्द्रकन्या स्थाणुं तपस्यन्तमधित्यकायाम् ।
अन्वास्त इत्यप्सरसां मुखेभ्यः श्रुतं मया मत्प्रणिधिः स वर्गः ॥१७॥

For through her father's command, Pārvatī (Nagendra's daughter) is waiting upon Lord Śiva, who is practising penance upon an upper ridge of Himādri; so have I heard from apsarasas' mouth; for they are my emissaries. (17).

तद्‌ गच्छ सिद्ध्यै कुरु देवकार्यमर्थोऽयमर्थान्तरभाव्य एव ।
अपेक्षते प्रत्ययमुत्तमं त्वां बीजाङ्कुरः प्रागुदयादिवाम्भः ॥१८॥

Then proceed, accomplish gods' business; for this business is to be accomplishes through another; for as a sprout from a seed requires water before it appears, so does it expect thee as the best cause. (18).

तस्मिन्सुराणां विजयाभ्युपाये तवैव नामास्त्रगतिः कृती त्वम् ।
अप्यप्रसिद्धं यशसे हि पुंसामनन्यसाधारणमेव कर्म ॥१९॥

For, the only means for subduing Hara is your arrow's

flight; for you are, indeed, blest; an extraordinary deed, though obscure, leads to man's success. (19).

सुराः समभ्यर्थयितार एते कार्यं त्रयाणामपि विष्टपानाम् ।
चापेन ते कर्म न चातिहिंस्रमहो बतासि स्पृहणीयवीर्यः ॥२०॥

For these gods are the snppliants; this business belongs to the three worlds, the deed wrought by thy bow is not very cruel. (20).

मधुश्च ते मन्मथ साहचर्यादसावनुक्तोऽपि सहाय एव ।
समीरणो नोदयिता भवेति व्यादिश्यते केन हुताशनस्य ॥२१॥

Spring, O Madana, thy ally is, though unbespoken; who ever doth command wind to help fire to blaze up?" (21).

तथेति शेषामिव भर्तुराज्ञामादाय मूर्ध्ना मदनः प्रतस्थे ।
ऐरावतास्फालनकर्कशेन हस्तेन पस्पर्श तदङ्गमिन्द्रः ॥२२॥

"So be it", said Madana, and started and honoured his master's command by receiving it on his head as a garland of favour. And Indra patted him with his hand, hardened by striking Airāvata. (22).

स माधवेनाभिमतेन सख्या रत्या च साशङ्कमनुप्रयातः ।
अङ्गव्ययप्रार्थितकार्यसिद्धिः स्थाण्वाश्रमं हैमवतं जगाम ॥२३॥

Accompanied by Spring, his esteemed friend, and by Rati in fear of peril, he wended his way to Śiva's Himavata Abode, by himself immolating. (23).

तस्मिन्वने संयमिनां मुनीनां तपःसमाधेः प्रतिकूलवर्ती ।
सङ्कल्पयोनेरभिमानभूतमात्मानमाधाय मधुर्जजृम्भे ॥२४॥

In that forest, Spring, opposed to the concentration for penances of the self-restrained sages, manifested himself, having taken the form which became the pride of the self-born. (24).

कुबेरगुप्तां दिशमुष्णरश्मौ गन्तुं प्रवृत्ते समयं विलङ्घ्य ।
दिग्दक्षिणा गन्धवहं मुखेन व्यलीकनिश्वासमिवोत्ससर्ज ॥२५॥

When the sun transited out of time, towards the quarter protected by Kubera, the Southern quarter experited from her mouth wind—the breath, as it were, of grief unbearable. (25).

असूत सद्यः कुसुमान्यशोकः स्कन्धात्प्रभृत्येव सपल्लवानि ।
पादेन नापैक्षत सुन्दरीणां सम्पर्कमासिञ्जितनूपुरेण ॥२६॥

Aśoka forthwith burgeoned forth flowers from the trunk onwards, in leaves encased, and did not expect contact of beautiful ladies' feet, with tinkling anklets dight. (26).

सद्यः प्रवालोद्गमचारुपत्रे नीते समाप्तिं नवचूतबाणे ।
निवेशयामास मधुर्द्विरेफान् नामाक्षराणीव मनोभवस्य ॥२७॥

When Spring had fashioned for Kāma, a new shaft with tender leaves for feathers, he forthwith incised upon it the letters as if of Madana's name in the form of bees. (27).

वर्णप्रकर्षे सति कर्णिकारं दुनोति निर्गन्धतया स्म चेतः ।
प्रायेण सामग्र्यविधौ गुणानां पराङ्मुखी विश्वसृजः प्रवृत्तिः ॥२८॥

Spite of richness of colour, from absence of fragrance, the Karṇikāra pains the mind. Averse is the Creator's activity from creating a totality of good qualities. (28).

बालेन्दुवक्राण्यविकासभावाद्बभुः पलाशान्यतिलोहितानि ।
सद्यो वसन्तेन समागतानां नखक्षतानीव वनस्थलीनाम् ॥२९॥

The very red Palāśa flowers shone like moon's curved crescent for want of blooming, as if they were the nail-marks by Vasanta, made on wood-land spots when he was united with them. (29).

लग्नद्विरेफाञ्जनभक्तिचित्रं मुखे मधुश्रीस्तिलकं प्रकाश्य ।
रागेण बालारुणकोमलेन चूतप्रवालोष्ठमलञ्चकार ॥३०॥

Spring's glory, manifesting on its forehead a tilaka-mark charming, with collyrium of bees thereto clinging with twi-light's colour delicate, embellished her lips in the form of tender mango-sprouts. (30).

मृगाः प्रियालद्रुममञ्जरीणां रजःकणैर्विघ्नितदृष्टिपाताः ।
मदोद्धताः प्रत्यनिलं विचेरुर्वनस्थलीर्मर्मरपत्रमोक्षाः ॥३१॥

The deer, their glances obstructed by Priyāla's pollen yellow, wandered with intoxication swollen windwards, towards the woodland spots, treading the leaves so as to make murmuring sounds. (31).

चूताङ्कुरास्वादकषायकण्ठः पुंस्कोकिलो यन्मधुरं चुकूज ।
मनस्विनीमानविघातदक्षं तदेव जातं वचनं स्मरस्य ॥३२॥

The male Koil with its throat hoarse with fresh mango blossom tasted, sweetly cooed, so that it bespake Cupid's mind. (32).

हिमव्यपायाद्विशदाधराणामापाण्डरीभूतमुखच्छवीनाम् ।
स्वेदोद्गमः किम्पुरुषाङ्गनानां चक्रे पदं पत्रविशेषकेषु ॥३३॥

Sweat appeared on ornamental paintings of Kimpuruṣa ladies; pallid was their complexion from the snow being rubbed away. (33).

तपस्विनः स्थाणुवनौकसस्तामाकालिकीं वीक्ष्य मधुप्रवृत्तिम् ।
प्रयत्नसंस्तम्भितविक्रियाणां कथञ्चिदीशा मनसां बभूवुः ॥३४॥

The hermits dwelling in the forest, seeing Spring's untimely onset, were somehow able to control their minds, with effort curbing their passions. (34).

तं देशमारोपितपुष्पचापे रतिद्वितीये मदने प्रपन्ने ।
काष्ठागतस्नेहरसानुविद्धं द्वन्द्वानि भावं क्रियया विवव्रुः ॥३५॥

When Cupid with his bow strung, appeared in the forest, accompanied by Rati, several couples exhibited their love by various appropriate actions—(love), which was mingled with heightened affection. (35).

मधु द्विरेफः कुसुमैकपात्रे पपौ प्रियां स्वामनुवर्तमानः ।
शृङ्गेण च स्पर्शनिमीलिताक्षीं मृगीमकण्डूयत कृष्णसारः ॥३६॥

The bee, following his mate, drank wine from the same flower-cup; and the black antelope scratched with his horns his mate who had her eyes closed by the pleasure of the touch. (36)

ददौ रसात्पङ्कजरेणुगन्धि गजाय गण्डूषजलं करेणुः ।
अर्धोपभुक्तेन बिसेन जायां सम्भावयामास रथाङ्गनामा ॥३७॥

The female elephant gave to its mate a mouthful of water, flavoured with the scent of the pollen of lotuses; and the cakravāka honoured his mate with a half-chewed lotus-stalk. (37).

गीतान्तरेषु श्रमवारिलेशैः किञ्चित्समुच्छ्वासितपत्रलेखम् ।
पुष्पासवाघूर्णितनेत्रशोभि प्रियामुखं किम्पुरुषश्चुचुम्बे ॥३८॥

A kinnara kissed the mouth of his beloved, which looked beautiful, as it whirled in consequence of her having guzzled floral wine and which had its ornamental paintings disfigured by drops of sweat caused by fatigue in the midst of a song. (38).

पर्याप्तपुष्पस्तबकस्तनाभ्यः स्फुरत्प्रवालोष्ठमनोहराभ्यः ।
लतावधूभ्यस्तरवोऽप्यवापुर्विनम्रशाखाभुजबन्धनानि ॥३९॥

The trees, too, were embraced by the bent branches, as if they were the arms of bride-like creepers, who possessed fully round breasts in the form of their big bunches of flowers, and whose lips in the form of their shining leaves looked lovely. (39).

श्रुताप्सरोगीतिरपि क्षणेऽस्मिन् हरः प्रसंख्यानपरो बभूव ।
आत्मेश्वराणां न हि जातु विघ्नाः समाधिभेदप्रभवो भवन्ति ॥४०॥

Śiva, although he heard the song of heavenly nymphs, set himself upon concentrating his mind upon himself, at this moment; obstacles impede not the mind's concentration of those who are Captains of their souls. (40).

लतागृहद्वारगतोऽथ नन्दी वामप्रकोष्ठार्पितहेमवेत्रः ।
मुखार्पितैकांगुलिसंज्ञयैव मा चापलायेति गणान् व्यनैषीत् ॥४१॥

Nandī who was at the entrance of the arbour, and who held a cane-staff in his left wrist, restrained the Gaṇas by making a sign to them by putting a finger in his mouth; thus commanding them to refrain from his chief. (41).

निष्कम्पवृक्षं निभृतद्विरेफं मूकाण्डजं शान्तमृगप्रचारम् ।
तच्छासनात्काननमेव सर्वं चित्रार्पितारम्भमिवावतस्थे ॥४२॥

By the command of Īśvara, the trees in the forest were not trembling, the birds were mute and the deer quiescent; the whole forest seemed to have all its activity drawn in a picture. (42).

दृष्टिप्रपातं परिहृत्य तस्य कामः पुरःशुक्रमिव प्रयाणे ।
प्रान्तेषु संसक्तनमेरुशाखं ध्यानास्पदं भूतपतेर्विवेश ॥४३॥

Kāma, avoiding his gaze like a king from the direction which has Śukra in its frontal part, dived into the place, where the lord of the goblin-hosts practised meditation, and on whose borders were branches of nameru trees interlacing one another. (43).

स देवदारुद्रुमवेदिकायां शार्दूलचर्मव्यवधानवत्याम् ।
आसीनमासन्नशरीरपातस्त्रियम्बकं संयमिनं ददर्श ॥४४॥

And Kāma, who was near shuffling off his mortal coil saw the self-restrained Hara who was squatting on an altar of Devadāru covered with tiger skin. (44).

पर्यङ्कबन्धस्थिरपूर्वकायमृज्वायतं सन्नमितोभयांसम् ।
उत्तानपाणिद्वयसन्निवेशात् प्रफुल्लराजीवमिवाङ्कमध्ये ॥४५॥

His body was steady owing to Paryaṅka posture; his shoulders were drooping and both his upturned hands rested in his lap, like blooming lotuses. (45).

भुजङ्गमोनद्धजटाकलापं कर्णावसक्तद्विगुणाक्षसूत्रम् ।
कण्ठप्रभासङ्गविशेषनीलां कृष्णत्वचं ग्रन्थिमतीं दधानम् ॥४६॥

God Śiva, whose matted locks were bound by a serpent and to whose ears was tied a rosary of Akṣa beads and who was wearing a knotted black antelope-skin, which was extremely blue owing to its contact with the blue colour of the neck of Śiva. (46).

किञ्चित्प्रकाशस्तिमितोग्रतारैर्भ्रूविक्रियायां विरतप्रसङ्गैः ।
नेत्रैरविस्पन्दितपक्ष्ममालैर्लक्ष्यीकृतघ्राणमधोमयूखैः ॥४७॥

His eyes, with their severe-looking pupils, were shining a little; his eyebrows ceased to dance; his eyelashes did not flicker and his eyes with their downward gaze, he rested on the tip of his nose. (47).

अवृष्टिसंरम्भमिवाम्बुवाहमपामिवाधारमनुत्तरङ्गम् ।
अन्तश्चराणां मरुतां निरोधान्निवातनिष्कम्पमिव प्रदीपम् ॥४८॥

He was like a cloud, not spilling down showers; like a lake without ripples; by controlling the inner winds, he was like a lamp unflickering in a windless place. (48).

कपालनेत्रान्तरलब्धमार्गैर्ज्योतिःप्ररोहैरुदितैः शिरस्तः ।
मृणालसूत्राधिकसौकुमार्यां बालस्य लक्ष्मीं ग्लपयन्तमिन्दोः ॥४९॥

He obscured the light of the crescent moon, more delicate than a lotus fibre, by rays of light upshooting from his head, making their way from the eye in his forehead. (49).

मनो नवद्वारनिषिद्धवृत्ति हृदि व्यवस्थाप्य समाधिवश्यम् ।
यमक्षरं क्षेत्रविदो विदुस्तमात्मानमात्मन्यवलोकयन्तम् ॥५०॥

Restraining his mind's activity in the nine outlets of the body, curbing his mind, which was controlled by concentration in his heart, he, who was known to the knowers of the Vedas as the eternal immutable, looking upon his soul in his own soul. (50).

स्मरस्तथाभूतमयुग्मनेत्रं पश्यन्नदूरान्मनसाऽप्यधृष्यम् ।
नालक्षयत्साध्वससन्नहस्तः स्रस्तं शरं चापमपि स्वहस्तात् ॥५१॥

Smara (the god of love) seeing the god (above described) Śiva, not from afar, who had odd eyes and who was unassailable even by the mind, did not mark that his bow and arrow dropped from his hand drooping through fright. (51).

निर्वाणभूयिष्ठमथास्य वीर्यं सन्धुक्षयन्तीव वपुर्गुणेन ।
अनुप्रयाता वनदेवताभ्यामदृश्यत स्थावरराजकन्या ॥५२॥

Then appeared Pārvatī, accompanied by sylvan deities who revived his valour almost lost by the beauty of her body. (52).

अशोकनिर्भर्त्सितपद्मरागमाकृष्टहेमद्युतिकर्णिकारम् ।
मुक्ताकलापीकृतसिन्धुवारं वसन्तपुष्पाभरणं वहन्ती ॥५३॥

Adorning herself with the flowers of spring in which the Aśoka flower spurned the Padmarāga gem, the karnikāra cried down the sheen of gold, and in which the Sinduvāra stood for clusters of pearls. (53).

आवर्जिता किञ्चिदिव स्तनाभ्यां वासो वसाना तरुणार्करागम् ।
पर्याप्तपुष्पस्तबकावनम्रा सञ्चारिणी पल्लविनी लतेव ॥५४॥

She was bent beneath the burden of her breasts and, draped in a garment crimson like the young Sun; she was like a moving plant covered with leaves, but beneath abundant bunches of flowers; (54).

स्रस्तां नितम्बादवलम्बमाना पुनः पुनः केसरदामकाञ्चीम् ।
न्यासीकृतां स्थानविदा स्मरेण मौर्वीं द्वितीयामिव कार्मुकस्य ॥५५॥

Frequently holding the girdle of Bakul-wreaths, slipping down from her lips, and deposited there as a second string of his bow, by the god of love, who knew the proper place for it; (55).

सुगन्धिनिश्वासविवृद्धतृष्णं बिम्बाधरासन्नचरं द्विरेफम् ।
प्रतिक्षणं सम्भ्रमलोलदृष्टिर्लीलारविन्देन निवारयन्ती ॥५६॥

Warding off the bee that hovered around her bimba-like lip whose thirst grew by her breath smelling sweat by the lotus, that adorned her hand, her eye rolling every moment through confusion; (56).

तां वीक्ष्य सर्वावयवानवद्यां रतेरपि ह्रीपदमादधानाम् ।
जितेन्द्रिये शूलिनि पुष्पचापः स्वकार्यसिद्धिं पुनराशशंसे ॥५७॥

On seeing her who was blameless in all her limbs, and

put to shame even Rati, Kāma once again, built up hopes of success in his venture in regard to the self-controlled Śiva. (57).

भविष्यतः पत्युरुमा च शम्भोः समाससाद प्रतिहारभूमिम् ।
योगात्स चान्तः परमात्मसंज्ञं दृष्ट्वा परं ज्योतिरुपारराम ॥५८॥

Umā came to the portal of the palace of Hara who was to be her future husband; and he ceased from Yaugic contemplation on perceiving within the light which is the highest soul. (58).

ततो भुजङ्गाधिपतेः फणाग्रैरधः कथञ्चिद्धृतभूमिभागः ।
शनैःकृतप्राणविमुक्तिरीशः पर्यङ्कबन्धं निबिडं बिभेद ॥५९॥

Then he, whose seat was somehow held by Śeṣa, gradually releasing his vital breath, broke his fast Paryaṅka-posture. (59).

तस्मै शशंस प्रणिपत्य नन्दी शुश्रूषया शैलसुतामुपेताम् ।
प्रवेशयामास च भर्तुरेनां भ्रूक्षेपमात्रानुमतप्रवेशाम् ॥६०॥

Then, bowing down to him, Nandī announced to him that Umā had arrived to wait upon him and on his indicating his consent by a flicker of his eyebrow, fetched her to Īśa. (60).

तस्याः सखीभ्यां प्रणिपातपूर्वं स्वहस्तलूनः शिशिरात्ययस्य ।
व्यकीर्यत त्र्यम्बकपादमूले पुष्पोच्चयः पल्लवभङ्गभिन्नः ॥६१॥

Then she, after bowing down to him, scattered at the feet of Tryambaka the flowers of spring, mixed with bits of leaves that had been gathered by her friends. (61).

उमाऽपि नीलालकमध्यशोभि विस्रंसयन्ती नवकर्णिकारम् ।
चकार कर्णच्युतपल्लवेन मूर्ध्ना प्रणामं वृषभध्वजाय ॥६२॥

Umā, too, disengaged the fresh Karṇikāra flower from her dark hair wherein it shone, and bowed down her head to Vṛṣabhadhvaja, while the leaf that adorned her ear slipped from it. (62).

अनन्यभाजं पतिमाप्नुहीति सा तथ्यमेवाभिहिता भवेन ।
नहीश्वरव्याहृतयः कदाचित्पुष्णन्ति लोके विपरीतमर्थम् ॥६३॥

And Śiva said to her, "Mayest thou obtain a husband unwavering in his love to thee; for the words of the great do not breed a sense that is false". (63).

कामस्तु बाणावसरं प्रतीक्ष्य पतङ्गवद्वह्निमुखं विविक्षुः ।
उमासमक्षं हरबद्धलक्ष्यः शरासनज्यां मुहुराममर्श ॥६४॥

Kāma, too, who was waiting for an opportunity to release his arrow, touched the string of his bow in the presence of Umā, and seemed to desire to enter the mouth of Fire, like a moth, making Hara his target. (64).

अथोपनिन्ये गिरिशाय गौरी तपस्विने ताम्ररुचा करेण ।
विशोषितां भानुमतो मयूखैर्मन्दाकिनीपुष्करबीजमालाम् ॥६५॥

Then Gaurī brought to Giriṣa, the anchorite, with her hand which had a red gleam, a rosary of lotus seeds of the lotuses that grew in the Ganges and that were dried by the rays of the sun. (65).

प्रतिग्रहीतुं प्रणयिप्रियत्वात् त्रिलोचनस्तामुपचक्रमे च ।
सम्मोहनं नाम च पुष्पधन्वा धनुष्यमोघं समधत्त बाणम् ॥६६॥

Śiva, who loved a supplicant, was about to accept the rosary, when the god of the flower-bow, placed upon his bow an unfailing shaft named Sammohana. (66).

हरस्तु किञ्चित्परिलुप्तधैर्यश्चन्द्रोदयारम्भ इवाम्बुराशिः ।
उमामुखे बिम्बफलाधरोष्ठे व्यापारयामास विलोचनानि ॥६७॥

Hara lost a little bit his firmness like the ocean at moon-rise, and directed his glance towards Umā's mouth with its Bimbalike lips. (67).

विवृण्वती शैलसुताऽपि भावमङ्गैः स्फुरद्बालकदम्बकल्पैः ।
साचीकृता चारुतरेण तस्थौ मुखेन पर्यस्तविलोचनेन ॥६८॥

Pārvatī, too, manifested her feeling with her limbs which were like flashing young Kadamba, and she stood bent sideways with bewildered eyes. (68).

अथेन्द्रियक्षोभमयुग्मनेत्रः पुनर्वशित्वाद्बलवन्निगृह्य ।
हेतुं स्वचेतोविकृतेर्दिदृक्षुर्दिशामुपान्तेषु ससर्ज दृष्टिम् ॥६९॥

Then Śaṅkara curbed the agitation of his senses with a strong will, as he was self-controlled, and looking for its cause, directed his eyes to the ends of the quarters. (69).

स दक्षिणापाङ्गनिविष्टमुष्टिं नतांसमाकुञ्चितसव्यपादम् ।
ददर्श चक्रीकृतचारुचापं प्रहर्तुमभ्युद्यतमात्मयोनिम् ॥७०॥

He saw the self-born (Kāma), resting his fist on the corner of his right eye, his shoulders bent, his left foot contracted and about to strike with an arrow placed upon his beautiful bow, fully bent. (70)

तपःपरामर्शविवृद्धमन्योर्भ्रूभङ्गदुष्प्रेक्ष्यमुखस्य तस्य ।
स्फुरन्नुदर्चिः सहसा तृतीयादक्ष्णः कृशानुः किल निष्पपात ॥७१॥

And from Śiva's third eye there shot up, all of a sudden, a flame of fire with its rays blazing up; his face, difficult to see as its eyebrow was (frightfully) wrinkled as he was greatly angered at disturbance in his penance. (71).

क्रोधं प्रभो संहर संहरेति यावद् गिरः खे मरुतां चरन्ति ।
तावत्स वह्निर्भवनेत्रजन्मा भस्मावशेषं मदनं चकार ॥७२॥

While the gods cried in heaven, "O Lord ! do curb your anger," the fire blazing from the eye of Bhava burnt Madana so that ashes were his only residue. (72).

तीव्राभिषङ्गप्रभवेण वृत्तिं मोहेन संस्तम्भयतेन्द्रियाणाम् ।
अज्ञातभर्तृव्यसना मुहूर्तं कृतोपकारेव रतिर्बभूव ॥७३॥

On Rati, the activity of whose senses was removed by the severe calamity, the swoon, that made her oblivious of her husband's death, seemed to confer an obligation for a while. (73).

तमाशु विघ्नं तपसस्तपस्वी वनस्पतिं वज्र इवावभज्य ।
स्त्रीसन्निकर्षं परिहर्तुमिच्छन्नन्तर्दधे भूतपतिः सभूतः ॥७४॥

Śiva, who was practising penance, having blasted him (i.e. Kāma) who was obstacle in his penance, like the thunderbolt a tree, wishing to avoid contact with a woman, disappeared with his hosts (Gaṇas). (74).

शैलात्मजाऽपि पितुरुच्छिरसोऽभिलाषं
व्यर्थं समर्थ्य ललितं वपुरात्मनश्च ।

सख्योः समक्षमिति चाधिकजातलज्जा
शून्या जगाम भवनाभिमुखी कथञ्चित् ॥७५॥

Pārvatī, too, considering as of no avail both the heart's desire of her high-souled father and her own graceful body, felt much ashamed of herself, now that all this happened in the presence of friends, was ill at ease, and moved homeward with great difficulty. (75).

सपदि मुकुलिताक्षीं रुद्रसंरम्भभीत्या
दुहितरमनुकम्प्यामद्रिरादाय दोर्भ्याम् ।
सुरगज इव बिभ्रत्पद्मिनीं दन्तलग्नां
प्रतिपथगतिरासीद् वेगदीर्घीकृताङ्गः ॥७६॥

Then Himādri led his daughter by her hand—(she) who shut her eyes out of fear of Rudra's wrath, and was on his way (homeward), and stretching his body, appeared like the elephant of the gods (Airāvata) carrying a lotus plant clinging to his tusks. (76).

———